IMAGES OF ENGLAND

AROUND
GRANGETOWN

IMAGES OF ENGLAND

AROUND
GRANGETOWN

JOHN M. O'NEILL

TEMPUS

Frontispiece: An unusually clear and magnificent view of the town in the 1960s. The River Tees is to the north and the steelworks is almost smokeless.

First published 2004

Tempus Publishing Limited
The Mill, Brimscombe Port,
Stroud, Gloucestershire, GL5 2QG
www.tempus-publishing.com

© John M. O'Neill, 2004

British Library Cataloguing in Publication Data.
A catalogue record for this book is available from the British Library.

ISBN 0 7524 3283 6

Typesetting and origination by Tempus Publishing Limited.
Printed in Great Britain.

Contents

Cleveland Hotel in the 1930s. Built in the 1850s inside the works, the Eston Junction Hotel originally provided accommodation for ironworks managers and their families. It was also a boon for thirsty blast furnace workers. The building later became a pay office for Dorman and Long & Co.

Acknowledgements

To those who supplied photographs or information and encouraged me to compile these for posterity, I tender my grateful thanks. Gratitude must especially be given to:

St Mary's Primary School Archives, Jim White, Dennis King, Sheila Barker, Joan Duckett, Kathleen Percival, Craig Hornby, Monsignor E. Wilcock, Gwen Wadwell, Eugene McElvaney, George Ayton, Elaine Meadows, Jim Keenan, Jean Turner, Peter Coleman, Kevin Murphy, Jim Rooney, Maureen Purvis, Tony Martin, Kathleen Potter, Agnes Mannix, Frank Clarke, John Field, Ken Lightfoot, Eric Kelly, Alan Thompson, Lisa Wiggins, Eddie Healy, Vera Robinson MBE, Bill Herlingshaw, Melda Keatley, Mary Fox, Vincent Fox, Clare Toomey, Bob Turner, Tess Pearsall, Corus PLC, Steve Dolphin, Ken Wanless, Jack Doyle, Dick Thomas, Ruth Swainston, Tony Walsh, John Carr, Lynne Waller, John Buckton, Dennis and Kathleen Dietz, Isolde Bradbury, John Smith, Brian Crowther, Patricia Millington and all those who contributed to the 'Grangetown In Times Past' website.

Introduction

Grangetown's early beginnings are well recorded but well worth repeating since it became such a unique town in 1881, designed to accommodate the vast numbers of ironworker immigrants as they flocked from all corners of the United Kingdom. Blended together under the canopy of Bolckow & Vaughan's industrial scene, it became a town of differing cultures, values and traditions which grew into a pleasant, hard-working place, isolated from its neighbouring towns, but quick to learn to adapt itself to the twentieth century and to tolerate its neighbours with a relaxed, steely sense of humour.

Its name was taken from Grange Farm, which was on nearby fields. Its particularly insular location was created by the branch railway line to Eston bordering the town in the west, with its bridge and subway, and the steelworks and river in the north. This geographical ghetto perhaps appeared a little forbidding to outsiders whilst inhabitants themselves often walked the mile or so to the entertainments and extra shopping facilities, which its neighbours in South Bank and Eston already possessed. The eight streets of Bessemer, Vaughan, Stapylton, Laing, Holden, Wood, Vickers and Cheetham – named after the men responsible for steel making – are sadly no more, but have been captured vividly in the images portrayed, along with its inimitable community.

It is a delight to see and enjoy the recorded moment of Victorian families and individuals posing in studios registering their newly-found affluence to the world and the later Edwardian period. We are extremely grateful to the photographers who toured the streets and recorded the life of people in Edwardian times – barefooted urchins playing with hoops, sticks, bogies, bikes, dolls and footballs, whilst their fathers sweated in blast furnaces, coke ovens and clattering mills and their mothers slaved to feed, clothe and care for their numerous offspring in the modern ironworker's cottage of a 'two up and two down'.

The revelation that an Athletic Stadium existed in Grangetown as far back as 1884 conveys a time of exciting leisure activities determined to be enjoyed by hard-working ironworkers and their families. The Stadium boasted a cinder track and facilities for cycling enthusiasts enjoyed by competitors from as far away as Derby, as well as a football club and pitches. The stories of cricket matches played out against the backdrop of gigantic blast furnaces and hunting and shooting for game suggests a scene almost reminiscent of a village in the country. Yet this was an area of farm and meadowland close to the sea where fishermen fished for salmon and everyone looked for shellfish down 'the slems'. Sea coal was sought in hard times and there were quite a few of those. The images of those who emigrated are testament to that.

The once famous Northern League football teams of Grangetown St Mary's and Grangetown Athletic exemplified the tremendous support shown towards this particular leisure activity, which more than once provided the gifted amateur with an opportunity to turn professional and created a status for many, comparable to today's footballing elite – without the remuneration of course.

The First World War is, of course, ever in the memory of the descendants of those who fought and died, and it is a privilege to pay tribute to the young men who served by recording a few examples of the brave and bold, in particular, recalling our own VC recipient and military medals gained in the campaign.

The exciting 1920s, as depicted on the cinema, seems far removed from Grangetown's photographs, where the growing of vegetables on allotments serve to remind us of the 'real' world, although there are occasional glimpses into that exciting world of music and dance when couples pose for a moment and the hint of a stylish dress is glimpsed. So perhaps its is the images from abroad that illustrate the real hardship suffered here when many families felt forced to emigrate to find work.

Although we know the 1930s was a depressing time for the steel industry, only the picture postcards seem to convey the sense of loneliness and despair that some must have felt and generate a kind of nostalgic longing for a time that appears so peaceful. The normal snaps of this era possess an informal, optimistic air, which is perhaps not so strange considering the advent of the mass produced box camera and the reluctance of people to acknowledge the possibility of a second World War so soon after the first, into which the town and its people were about to be engulfed. This was also a time of expansion; the excellent Eston Urban District Council supplied new housing for an ever-increasing population.

Uniforms once again filled the streets in the 1940s, and people are pictured in happy poses – all seemingly ready to participate in a new adventure – united once again to face new circumstances, different situations, form lasting friendships and in many circumstances, forge lasting marriages which in turn created a new set of Grangetown citizens. The forties rationing period, during which goods and clothes were scarce, are echoed in the distinctive style and dress of a generation who were increasingly aware of fashion. In the 1950s, youth began to breathe new life into the market after the scarcities of the war period and experimented with stylish outfits paid for by the new affluence which came from full employment.

Previous Grangetown books have revealed facts but have contained few illustrations or images. I have been lucky enough to be able to collect these images through contact with other family researchers and I feel privileged to have shared in their memories and pleasantly surprised that so many evocative images still exist. I hope you enjoy them as much as I have enjoyed discovering them.

one

Victorian Times

CLEVELAND STEEL WORKS.

MESSRS. BOLCKOW, VAUGHAN & Co., LTD., in making known these Regulations, hereby express their determination to see them strictly followed.

1. Every Workman employed in these Works is required to be at his work at the time appointed by his respective foreman and on his omitting to do so, and thereby neglecting his work, he will incur a fine of not less than Five Shillings.

2. Every Workman neglecting to write on his Time-board, with his time, the name of the article or articles he has been working at during the day, he will be fined for each offence, Sixpence.

3. Any Workman who does not return his own Time-board at the office when done work on the Saturday evening previous to the pay, with his full time for the week written thereon, to be fined Sixpence.

4. Any Workman leaving his candle burning, or neglecting to shut his gas cock, to be fined One Shilling.

5. Any Workman taking the tools of another, to be fined One Shilling.

6. Any Workman giving in more time than he has worked, to be fined Five Shillings.

7. Any Workman leaving his work without giving sufficient notice to his respective foreman, so that another may be appointed to fill his situation, shall be fined Five Shillings, or any Workman detected not finishing his work to the satisfaction of his employers or their agents shall, in addition to the above penalty, forfeit his wages on such work.

8. Any Workman found damaging the machinery or property of his employers, or wasting any materials belonging to them, either through carelessness or design, shall be fined Twenty Shillings It is moreover expected that every Workman having charge of any particular piece of machinery, furnace, or any instrument whatever, shall see the same is in proper order, or give due notice that the contrary is the case, so that as little interruption as possible may be offered to the work in repairing it, on neglecting to do so, he shall be fined Five Shillings.

9. All persons are strictly prohibited from bringing strangers into the works and any one found doing so, shall be fined Five Shillings.

10. Anyone bringing ale, wine or spirits into the works, will be fined Five Shillings, and no Smoking will be allowed during work hours, under a penalty of One Shilling for each offence.

11. Any person misplacing any iron or other objects, and depositing ashes, slag, clay, &c, in any other place than that appointed by his employers or their agents, shall be fined Two Shillings and Sixpence.

12. Any person wishing to quit the service of the Company, must give notice of his intention on the pay-day, fourteen days previous to the time he wishes to leave, or forfeit any wages which may be due to him, and render himself liable to be prosecuted. On the other hand, workmen may demand an equal notice from the Company, unless they have been guilty of misconduct.

13. Any person leaving the employ of the Company must bring the key of his house to the Office on the day he ought to quit, and no wages will be paid to him until he does so.

14. Anyone striking another, or quarrelling, shall be fined Two Shillings and Sixpence, or, in case of dispute, their masters or agents to be appealed to.

15. Any person leaving or entering the Works by any other than the proper gateways, shall forfeit Ten Shillings.

16. Any person using disrespectful language to the Manager, Foreman, or Overlooker, and refusing to obey them, will be fined Five Shillings.

17. The Masters reserve to themselves the right of increasing the amount of fines on the offences being repeated, and shall also, in extreme cases, apply for the assistance of the Magistrates.

FINALLY, all Fines to go to a Fund for the relief of Distressed Workmen, or any Workman who may receive injury on the Works.

BOLCKOW, VAUGHAN & Co., Ld.

Above: An early drawing of the steel works, the reason for Grangetown's existence. An increased workforce was essential for operating the newly designed steel-making plants and furnaces required in a new town.

Left: The Rules and Regulations of Bolckow, Vaughan & Co. Ltd.

Opposite below: Eston Junction, *c.* 1895: Commonly known as 'The Branch' and Eston Junction, this picture shows Stapylton Villas in the left-hand corner allowing the visual impact of the eighty-eight ironworkers' cottages to be captured in the centre of the picture against the backcloth of the towering blast furnaces. To the right is Cleveland Villas, the large group of houses that precede the twelve railway cottages. It's hard to believe that cricket matches were played against this background.

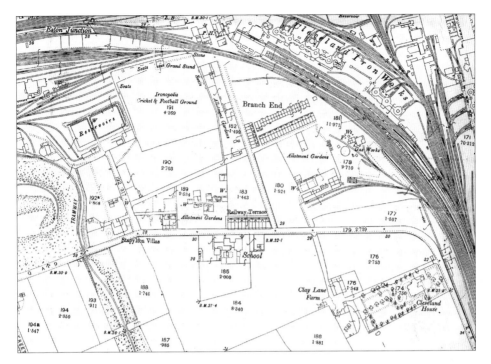

Above: Branch End Map in 1895. Branch End or Eston Junction are synonymous terms for that part of the railway line which existed to convey the ironstone from the mines of Eston Hills to its furnaces and beyond. Originally the line stretched along the riverside from Middlesbrough to South Bank, Low Lackenby and Warrenby and roads were few. Travel was restricted to the railway for many years and the black path to the coast was always preferable until the Trunk Road was built in the 1920s. Hence the decision to house the workers of the newly created Eston Works in the 1870s meant a new town east of the branch line to Eston and in 1881 the eight streets of Grangetown began.

Railway Terrace, *c.* 1895. This terrace contained the station master, railway porters, signalmen, shunters, ticket collectors, agents, telegraph clerks etc. (and their families) employed by the North Eastern Railway.

Low Lackenby Workmen. Second from right on the back row is James Murphy, an Irish immigrant from County Monaghan who saw 'the fires in the sky' over Teesside and married Ann Ruddy in South Bank, before settling in Grangetown with his family. His children followed suit by emigrating to Chicago in the 1920s where his grandson Kevin became a writer – perhaps inspired by his grandfather's dramatic turns of phrase.

Above: Bolckow Terrace, *c.* 1900. Around the corner from Branch End past the Works Manager's Cleveland House, lay Bolckow Terrace, a group of twenty-five cottages, which were originally the homes of selected employees of Bolckow and Vaughan such as locomotive drivers, roll turners, foremen, boiler smiths, gas fitters, engine fitters, analytical chemists, carpenters and traffic agents. Holme Beck ran alongside the Eston Branch Railway line and was soon polluted.

Right: Family in 5 Bolckow Terrace, *c.* 1900. John Livingstone, a foreman at the ironworks, is pictured with his wife and family outside their Bolckow Terrace home surrounded by foliage we would now find hard to imagine. He can be seen with his fellow workers in the next image.

Blast furnace workers, *c.* 1900. Standing on the extreme right is John Livingstone working as a blast Furnace pig iron foreman alongside a bowler-hatted manager, seated nearby. The gentleman in the forefront appears to be holding a tool indicative of the nature of his position in the gang and the man second from the right in the front row looks suspiciously like James Murphy, pictured earlier with the Low Lackenby Workers.

Above: Crane Men, *c.* 1900. John Thomas, front row second from the right, is pictured with Bolckow & Vaughan's workforce in the early part of the twenty-first century. The faces and poses are familiar to their workplace, which became the chief supplier of iron and steel in the western world.

Right: The Sport's Day Programme from 1890. Mr Moss, Head Teacher of the recently built Board School, was the prize giver at this annual event on the Jubilee Field on which everyone must have celebrated similarly in 1887 for Queen Victoria's Golden Jubilee. Competitors from as far away as Darlington and Sunderland travelled by rail to participate. It must have been a very grand occasion with the local Brass Band playing and ladies and gentlemen waltzing in the evening sunlight.

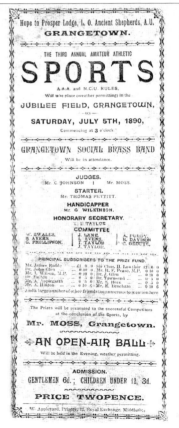

Above: The One-Armed Runner. John Watson lost his arm as a young boy of seven when it was trapped between the buffers of a line of trucks as he was crossing to watch a cricket match near Eston Junction. As his mother helped him remove his coat after the game, she was shocked to see his arm hanging on by a thread. Immediately, the local GP was summoned, who performed the amputation on the kitchen table. Undaunted by his handicap, John became a proficient runner and earned a reputation as a sprinter. The polished table in the parlour of 24 Bolckow Terrace displayed trophies for all to see and they were never stolen.

Above: Durham Light Infantry Regiment
Recruits, *c.* 1895. A DLI tug-of-war team
photographed at their barracks, somewhere
in the North East. Bottom right is Michael
Traynor (1875-1952) from Holden Street,
Grangetown, who had a considerable
reputation for strength.

Right: Michael Traynor, *c.* 1894. This early
picture was taken soon after recruitment,
when he joined up to escape the
unemployment faced by many at this time in
Bolckow & Vaughan's ironworks. He fought
in the Boer War after serving with his
regiment in India, where he acquired a taste
for curry. He was a prolific artist and
craftsman, possessing considerable skill and
worked in brass, wood and Whitby jet,
carving works of art and intricate ornaments.

Opposite below: Locomotive Normanby,
c. 1900. William Tonkin of Vickers Street
poses nonchalantly in his bowler before an
early locomotive built by Black &
Hawthorne of Gateshead, dated 1881.

Above: The McNicholas Family in 1898. James McNicholas, a labourer, from County Mayo and Mary Kenny from Armagh were living in 64 Vaughan Street with children Annie, Mary, Margaret, John, Alice and James in 1898. Winifred was born after this photograph was taken. Two of the children became teachers in St Mary's and John emigrated to the USA in the 1920s and became a successful businessman.

Left: The Sleight family, *c.* 1890. Along with thousands of similar migrant workers, the Sleights of Lincolnshire typified the extent to which families were prepared to travel. Many were keen to sample the opportunities afforded by the newfound industrial wealth engendered by the iron-making entrepreneurs in this newly created 'gold rush' area. The story goes that Westoby, the bearded gentleman wheelwright pictured, used his last shillings to put his family on the train to North Yorkshire and set off to walk the 100 miles to this thriving community. His first job as a joiner was in the ironworks of Skinningrove. He later practised his trade in the Cleveland Works area where most of his family eventually stayed. His son, John William (Bill), became the pikelet man so familiar to the small towns around Grangetown. He lived in the White House in Eston. From left to right, back row: Arthur (seated), John, Westoby and Charles. Front row: Walter, wife Jane Beel, Lucy and Thomas.

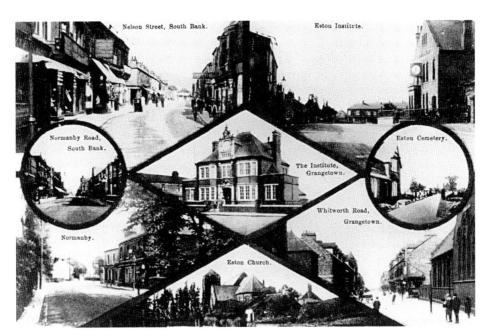

Above: Views of Grangetown and surrounding area, *c.* 1900. A delightfully designed postcard of the era illustrating the diverse nature of the area with its notable buildings and streets. The Literary Institute, also called the Mechanic's Institute, was built in 1884 as a place of recreation and education. It later became the home of the Grangetown Boy's Club.

Right: Eston Grange, *c.* 1900. John Field, an overseer at Bolckow & Vaughan's ironworks, and his wife are pictured here with children James, Mary, Richard Henry, Lillian and baby Cecilia. Eston Grange was a row of 24 terraced houses on the eastern side of the Works facing the sea. It was known locally as 'Cockle Row' because of its proximity to the 'Slems' – a term used to describe the marshland near the coast.

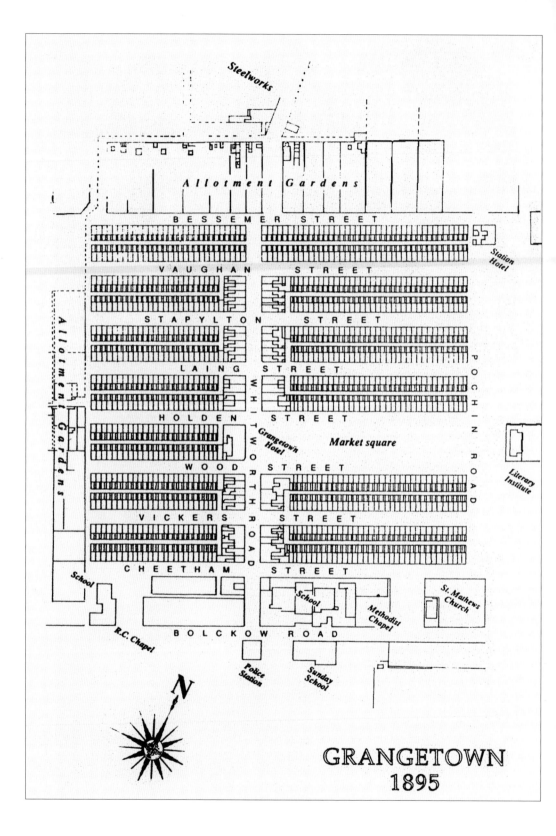

GRANGETOWN
1895

Left: Reverend Canon J.J. Nolan was one of the most influential parish priests and promoters of education in the days of Grangetown St Mary's inception in 1884. He was responsible for guiding the school and its governors as well as for caring for the lives of his own parishioners in South Bank. His efforts and skills in education were not restricted to his own flock. He was on hand to inform and was often seen in the nearby Board School.

Right: Reverend Fr Patrick Cronin, *c.* 1900. This young man replaced Canon James Nolan as parish priest in St Mary's but stayed for just four years before being replaced by the dynamic Fr Bernard Kelly.

Opposite: An early Map of Streets dated 1895. The building of Grangetown's streets began in 1881 to provide Bolckow & Vaughan with a permanent labour force to cope with the increased production which the recently completed Eston Works demanded and to cope with the overcrowded housing conditions experienced in places like nearby Eston Junction and Eston Grange. A new town of eight streets containing 768 houses emerged, which expanded rapidly southwards to reach Eston with an increasing population until the latter part of the twentieth century.

Esther Pattison, daughter of a Whitesmith in Richmond, met and married the bricklaying Irishman, Patrick Golden from County Mayo in St Peter's RC church in South Bank. She settled in Laing Street with her family.

Mary Anne Lynne, c. 1895. Mary was a devoted Salvationist who later married William Tonkin, a foreman in the railway department section of Bolckow & Vaughan's Works. They lived in Vickers Street. The photograph was taken in South Shields.

Annie Gainford, of 43 Holden Street, was a daughter of George, pictured here as a fashionable young girl of the late 1890s. She married Ernie Bradbury of South Bank and ran a corner shop in nearby North Ormesby. They had three daughters.

George Gainford of Monaghan, Middlesbrough, Witton Park, South Bank and Grangetown, followed the pattern of so many Irish emigrants when he left his Carrickmacross birthplace after the potato famine of 1845–48, to work as a labourer in the ironworks of Bolckow & Vaughan. He married Bridget Callaghan in Middlesbrough and fathered three daughters, all of whom married local men.

Bolckow Road and Board School, *c.* 1900. The impressive building on the corner is the
Town Hall, built in 1886, which was radically altered in the 1930s by the installation of
plate glass windows to display Brown's Shop furniture and furnishings. The intricate
wrought iron fencing on each house is a joy to see. The lady, we believe, is the wife
of Doctor Andrew Steele, a well-known local GP.

Market Square facing Grangetown Hotel, *c.* 1900. An impressive building which catered for
the needs of Bolckow & Vaughan's directors and managers in earlier times.

Whitworth Road facing south, *c.* 1900. It was a wonderfully evocative postcard of the time that captures the atmosphere of the main street, as it was known. The police station faced the street as if to keep a watchful eye on proceedings, which was apparently necessary in the early days of Grangetown's inception, when 'shebeening' played its part in encouraging riotous behaviour towards 'blacklegs', miners and others. The speedy construction of this imposing edifice soon restored things to normal.

Whitworth Road facing North, *c.* 1900. The presence of bicycles and horse-drawn vehicles and the barber's pole depict a bustling scene of the period.

Five views of Grangetown's early days, *c.* 1900.

Grangetown and District Social Club, *c.* 1900. A building which still survives today and a club, which has served the people faithfully for over a century.

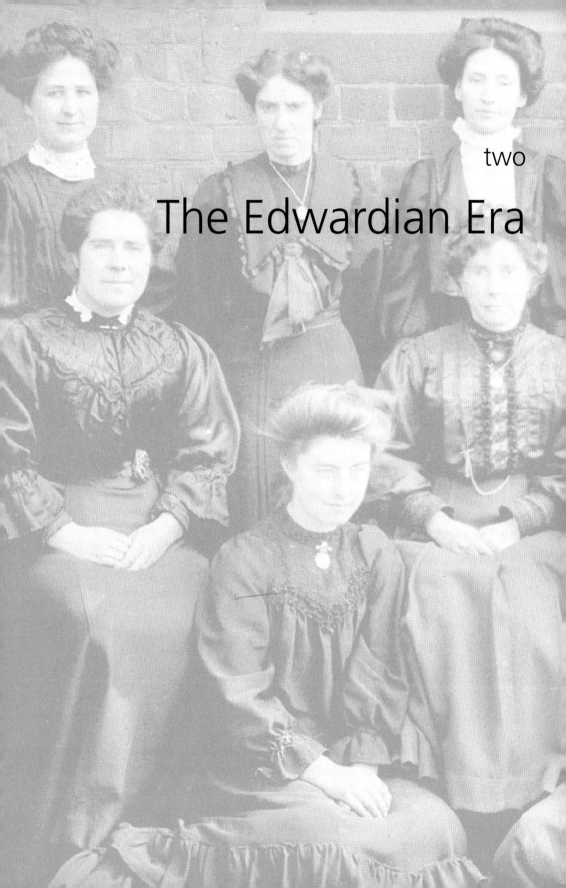

two

The Edwardian Era

St Mary's staff, *c.* 1905. From left to right, back row: Kate or Lizzie Gribbin, -?-, Ellen Mahon, -? -, Lucy Toomey. Middle row: Mrs Reed, Mrs Bridget Fox, Miss McNicholas. Front row: Miss Pearson(?), Margaret McNicholas (Walsh).

St Mary's Mixed Infants, *c.* 1905. A class of twenty-eight pupils squint at the camera alongside teachers Miss McQuade (right), and a younger teacher who may be Miss Ethel Pearson (left).

Above: St Mary's Class III, *c.* 1905. The teacher is Margaret McNicholas, later Walsh. The children identified to date are three Thomas children in the centre.

Left: St Mary's Infant Staff, *c.* 1905. Left to right: Abigail Cooney, Miss McQuade, Helena Jane Pearson. Seated at the front is Miss Ethel Pearson. These sisters left the school soon after this photograph was taken, to work in York. Ethel married Mr Wilcock and her son became a priest in the Leeds Diocese.

Above: St Mary's Gala *c.* 1905. A concert photograph of schoolchildren dressed in sashes and costumes reminiscent of the land of Erin. Two boy pipers are dressed in costume with kits and a harp is held up in the centre. This type of performance was often used to raise funds for the school and the church.

Left: St Mary's church, *c.* 1905. This beautiful church was built in 1905 to replace the small chapel on Bolckow Road, which doubled up as a school. Its construction was due to the efforts of the parishioners and the unstinting efforts of the Revd Fr Bernard Kelly who served the parish for nearly twenty-six years until his death in 1928. He became the site foreman on this magnificent edifice, which was sadly demolished in 1988.

Opposite above: Grangetown Athletic Club Runners. Pictured here is the accomplished amateur sprinter John Watson holding a starting pistol and trainer Mr Spencer with fourteen Grangetown boys, practising their skills before the great day when they would compete for prize money – enough incentive for any boy! The names written on the reverse of photograph are, back row: ? Craggs, Evan Thomas, Fly Burke, Willie Simpson, and George Watson (second from the right). Middle row: ? Siffle, Charlie Cordery, Tulty Watson, ? Jarret, ? Mahon. Front row: ? Green, ? Donachy, ? Singer. Charlie Cordery is the blonde-haired boy third from right.

Grangetown Athletic Club.

Amateur . . *. . Athletic* SPORTS, Saturday, . . July 22, 1905.

100 Yds. FLAT RACE H'CAP FOR SCHOLARS.

1st PRIZE value £1.

Silver Watch & Chain, presented by R.R.

SUPPLIED BY

R. RICHARDSON, The Presentation Jeweller, SUSSEX STREET, MIDDLESBRO'.

Above: Prize Ticket £1, in 1905.

Altar boys, *c.* 1904. Peter Mahon, who was born in 1893, is standing far left in the back row. He is the only boy known on this photograph taken in the school playground. He became the headmaster of St Mary's School in 1931 after teaching at the Grangetown Board School in the 1920s.

A successful young team, *c.* 1910. They are pictured here displaying their magnificent Championship Shield.

Grangetown Wednesday Football Team in 1908. The team were so named because they played on Wednesdays. Their numbers perhaps included shop workers, free to play on Wednesday afternoons and shift workers from the Bolckow & Vaughan's steelworks.

Cleveland Hotel Football Team, *c.* 1910. George Watson of Bolckow Terrace sitting with the ball at his feet, lived a stone's throw from this hotel, which catered for the needs of thirsty blast furnace workers and was also a residential hotel for visitors.

The Walsh family of Bessemer Street. Back row: Tom, Paddy, Jim, Andrew. Middle row: Mary, Mr Andrew Walsh, John, Mrs Margaret Walsh, Winnie. Front row: Michael, Joe and Bill. Maggie Walsh, later Pattison, was born in 1909; her mother Margaret Tierney was living in 117 Bessemer Street in 1887, when Maggie married Andrew of 43 North Street in South Bank in St Mary's Chapel in Grangetown. Andrew Walsh was born in the Swinford parish of County Mayo in 1856 and his mother was a McManus.

Vickers Street facing East, *c.* 1908. Harry Scutt of No.50 sent this postcard to friends in York in 1908. Pochin Road School is just visible in the background.

Grangetown's first Fire Engine, *c.* 1910. Harry Phillipson is the fireman on display pictured with the first horse-drawn Fire Engine that was stationed in Cheetham Street behind Whitworth Road Council Offices.

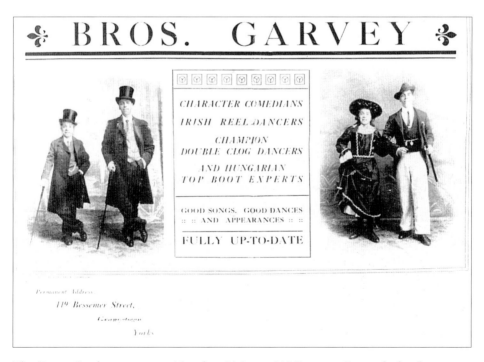

The Garvey Brothers, an enterprising duo. Living at 119 Bessemer Street, the brothers advertised their skills to the world on a special hand-printed bill that has fortunately survived the test of time.

Pochin Road Infants Classroom, *c.* 1911. A classroom scene of the time, revealing the distinct separation between boys and girls in the same room.

Grangetown Board School children, *c.* 1911. The Board Schools, opened in 1884, had accommodation for 900 scholars. John Moss was headmaster, Miss Duncan was headmistress and Miss Alexander was the infants' mistress. There was fierce resentment from some pupils who hated paying for their tuition. Mr Moss was later replaced by Josiah Huss as headmaster. Mr Huss is pictured here on the right.

Eston Junction in 1912. A group of children pose beside their chalk-walled graffiti. We could perhaps speculate on the owner of the initials J.M. and the possible surname. Families with the names of Magnier, Maloney, Manix, McAleer, McCabe, McCann, McCardle, McCarthy, McCaul, McCleary, McCoy, McCracken, McGowan, McGurk, McKenna, McMaura, McNamee, Meskill, Mohan, Morris, Murphy and Murray all occupied homes in this small hamlet. We could, however, still be wrong.

Eston Junction, again in 1912. Another group of 'branch' kids children line up against the chalked goalposts of a walled terraced block in Eston Junction which housed over 100 families in its heyday.

GRANGETOWN ATHLETIC FOOTBALL CLUB.
(1910-11).
MEMBERS OF NORTHERN LEAGUE.)

Grangetown
* Athletic *
ASSOCIATION
Football Club
(Members of Northern
. League).

SEASON 1912-13.

Patrons
Herbert Samuel, Esq., M P.
Penry Williams, Esq., M.P.
James Eadie, Esq.

President
John Turner, Esq.

Rep. & Hon. Treasurer
Mr. James Douglass

Hon. Secretary
Mr. Fred Williams,
Grangetown, Yorks

Committee
Messrs. G. Kay
J. McKeown
R. Phillipson
W. Phillipson
D. Thomas
C. Wills
J. Hetteron
D. Cowhig
C. Hierons
E. Reardon
J. Hetherington
J. Heath

Chairman
Mr. Josiah Huss

Captain
Mr. Robt. H. Simpson

Vice-Captain
Mr. T. Reardon

Trainer
Mr. T. Feeney

Colours
Royal Blue & White Vertical
Striped Jerseys, and Navy
Blue Knickers.

Ground
Recreation Ground,
Grangetown.

Above: Grangetown Athletic FC from the 1910/11 season. Pictured with their coach, trainers and supporters are Goalkeeper Harry Thomas; Backs Kennedy and Simpson; Halfbacks Henry, Davies and Jim Thomas; Forwards Murtha, Neesham, Reardon, Hanlon and Jones.

Left: Membership Book of the 1912/13 Season. This small leather-bound book, containing all the fixtures for the forthcoming season was found in an allotment shed many years later. Names listed include some of those seen in the image above.

Left: School friends from 1910. Nora Golden of Laing Street and Annie McKenna (seated) of Bessemer Street pose in a studio shortly before Annie's emigration to the USA where she married Lloyd Thomas of Omaha in 1911.

Right: 'Big Din' Healy in 1910. At almost the same time as the two girls were having their photograph taken, Dennis 'Big Din' Healy poses outside his home, also in Bessemer Street, with his two sons Jack and Dennis, after his wife Sarah (Burt) had tragically died, aged twenty-eight. He later married a widow, Bella Purcell, from the same street who, unable to cope with young Jack, allowed him to be sent to the Healy farm in Ireland. Sarah's mother, 'Granny' Burt, brought up Dennis until 'Big Din' died in 1926. Jack returned to the area later as a young man and was an amateur comedian on the stage.

Whitworth Road on Coronation Day, 22 June 1911. A well-preserved paper serviette of 1911 included the sports programme arranged for 22 June 1911 to celebrate the coronation of King George V. Activities included catching a greasy pig (an activity open to married women only) and catching a hen (ladies only). Events took place on the Jubilee Field.

Whitworth Road in 1911. The main street is decked out in bunting ready for the occasion.

Below: Argyle Road, *c.* 1910. Almost a rural scene depicting the Social Club on the left, the fields on the right and the rear of the police station.

Colley's Butcher Shop, *c.* 1912. Ted Colley pictured second left, poses outside his newly acquired butcher's shop in Whitworth Road.

Above: Grangetown St Mary's Girls, *c.* 1900. A unique photograph which features Reverend Fr Kelly and curate seated with teaching staff and the girls of the parish. From left to right: -?-, -?-, Miss M. McNicholas, Curate?, Reverend Fr Kelly, Miss Gribbin, Miss McQuade and Lucy Toomey.

Left: Toomey's Corner Shop, *c.* 1910. Mr Tooney established this tobacco and confectionery shop in 1909. It later became Davison's Corner Shop and, later still, became Richardson's. The boy outside is probably Richard Toomey who, in the 1930s, taught at the Board School and Sir William Worsley School.

Opposite below: Children pose in Holden Street, *c.* 1912. The owner of the picture, Amy Brien (of the USA), has supplied the names. Standing are: Louisa Heath, Frances Shaddack, Blanche Saddler, Amy Brien, Jane Ward, J. Gatiss, -?-, -?-, -?-, John Duffy, -?-. John Duffy from County Mayo became a local fisherman. His boat, *Top O' The Morning*, was kept at the local breakwater.

Above: Bessemer Street, *c.* 1912. Street games are temporarily suspended as the children pose for the photographer. Third from the left is barefooted Patrick Burke. Leaning on the handlebars of a large bicycle is Johnna McAuliffe and, standing in the doorway of No.77, is Mrs Simpson. On the reverse of this postcard is the handwritten name, James Traynor. Mr Traynor was a well-known cobbler who plied his trade from his house shop in one of the nearby streets.

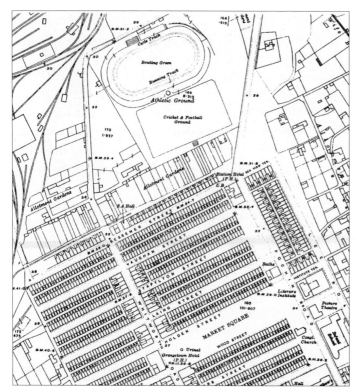

Left: A map of the Grangetown Stadium in 1915. Built in 1884, the stadium was a magnificent venue for cyclists from all over the country where, soon after alighting from the nearby Railway Station, they regularly competed in events. Local children earned many a halfpenny for carrying a spare wheel to the track. It was demolished during the First World War.

Below: Cycling Club, *c.* 1912. George Lightfoot, a newspaper vendor of Whitworth Road, is sitting in the front row on the left.

The Cycling Club at rest, *c.* 1912. This familiar leisure activity mirrored the pursuits seen in the rest of society. Here, the club are seen in a local beauty spot, which looks like the valley gardens of Saltburn. George Lightfoot is now second from the right.

Grangetown's St Mary's FC. In 1914, St Mary's were the season's North Riding Amateur Cup Winners when they defeated West Hartlepool Expansion by two goals to nil. The players pictured are: ? Vickers, Billy Noteyoung, Dai Thomas, Jim Thomas, ? Whelan, ? Haining, ? Jones, ? Hanlon, ? Evans, ? Collins, staff and the remainder of the squad.

The Victory Celebration in 1913. Celebrations occurred when Middlesbrough's proposed case to extend its boundaries was defeated. Middlesbrough hoped to absorb Eston and Normanby's industrial land, but was prevented from doing so by the House of Commons. Councillor Robert Brown returned home a hero from Grangetown station to receive a rapturous welcome by 7,000 people who listened to his address in the Market Square despite the drizzling rain and roared with delight and approval at his words. The decorated platform on which he stood contained messages such as 'Victory is Ours' pinned to the draperies.

The Market Square Medal of 1914. This was struck to honour the pledge made by the directors of Bolckow, Vaughan & Co. when they gave the Market Square to the people of Grangetown in a speech by Sir Johnson-Ferguson Bart on 29 July 1914. It was a gift of land highly appreciated by the townspeople, and fiercely defended in later years.

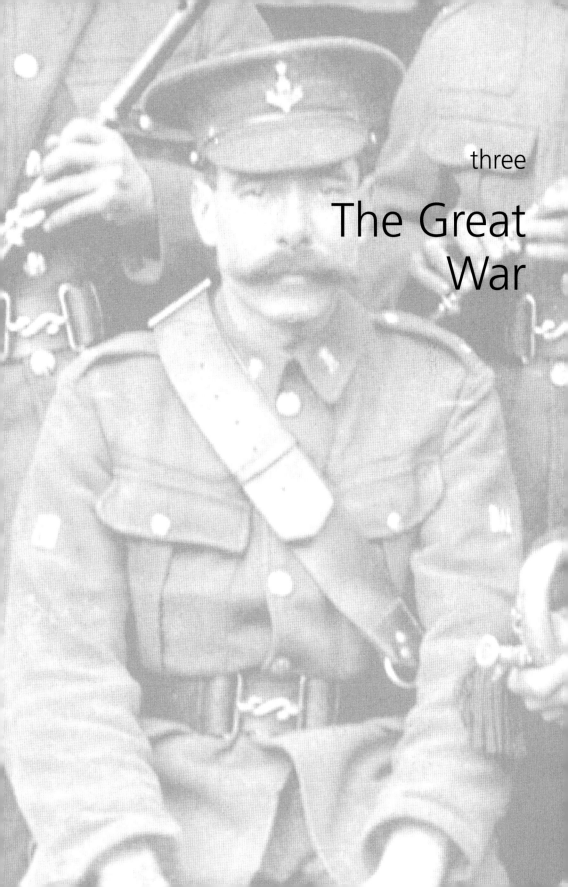

three

The Great
War

Pte William 'Twig' Short VC. William Short of Vaughan Street was awarded the VC posthumously for conspicuous bravery at Munster Alley near Pozières on 6 August 1916, by bombing the enemy with great gallantry. Despite being severely wounded in the foot he stayed in a trench adjusting detonators and straightening the pins of bombs for his comrades. He died before he could be carried out of the trench. An obelisk memorial was erected to his name in the Market Square and now stands in Eston Cemetery.

Pte Jack Kennedy of Vaughan Street. Jack was awarded the Military Medal for holding a trench against an enemy onslaught. He was badly wounded in the process. He carried enemy bullets in his body until his death some forty years later in Vaughan Street.

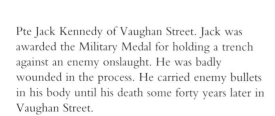

George Lightfoot of Whitworth Road. George Lightfoot was part of the King's Own Yorkshire Light Infantry. He survived and was able to return to his newsagency, which his mother had continued in his absence. His brother Herbert did not return.

Young Volunteers from 1914. Fresh from the football field, Dai Thomas and his best friend Bill Noteyoung pose in a studio for a cleverly designed propaganda postcard of the time. They joined the 7th Battalion Yorkshire Regiment, which later became the Green Howard's Regiment. They both returned home safely.

Peter Higgins of Bessemer Street.
Private Peter Higgins of the 7th Battalion
Yorkshire Regiment died on 1 July 1916,
aged twenty-seven years. He was the son of
John and Mary Higgins of 67 Bessemer
Street, Grangetown.

John Fox of Bolckow Road. 2nd-Lt John Fox of
the 5th Battalion Connaught Rangers died on
18 November 1917, aged twenty-two years. He
was the son of Councillor John and Bridget Fox of
Bolckow Road, Grangetown.

Jim O'Brien of Laing Street with his wife
Maggie in 1914.

George Frederick Watson of Bolckow Terrace.
George was killed in the Battle of the Somme in
1916, at the age of twenty-one. He was a young
sportsman who captained the Cleveland Hotel
Soccer Team in Eston Junction and was an
amateur runner. Like many other parents, his
mother never recovered from the loss of her son.
He is still mourned by his sisters who attend the
cenotaph service every year in Grangetown.

Adelphi Hotel, Harrogate.
The hotel was a source of
employment for a number
of Grangetown girls, Liz
and Mary Burke are
amongst the women posing
in the grounds of the Hotel.

Mrs Newton of Bessemer
Street in 1914. Whilst
families were losing their
young men to the training
grounds and battlefields of
France, Mrs Newton posed
with her grandchildren in
the yard of her Bessemer
Street home.

Above: St Mary's staff pose in the playground, *c.* 1914. Lucy Toomey (positioned front left) lived in a large house in Bolckow Road next to the police station until her death.

Right: George Ayton of Vickers Street, photographed in 1914. George William Ayton of the Green Howards' Regiment lost an eye during a battle.

Above: Ladies at leisure in 1918. Pictured are Bolckow, Vaughan & Co.'s Ladies' Soccer Team, which started early in the war years. From left to right, back row: Emily Milner, Amelia Farrell, Greta Kirk and Violet Sharples. Front row: Elizabeth Powell, Mary Mohan, Mercy Page, Winnie McKenna, Gladys Reece, Olive Percival and Anne Wharton.

Opposite above: Ladies at work. Mrs Purvis (top row, second left) and Mrs Nora Cave of Laing Street (front row, left) along with their female colleagues, took on a male role when they were employed at Bolckow & Vaughan's Works, during this revitalised period of steel production. Their enthusiasm and dedicated effort during the war produced new records for steel manufacture and contributed in no small way to the war effort.

Right: Winnie McKenna. A portrait of Winnie McKenna, the female 'Wilf Mannion' of the day, who played for England. She was born in the shadow of the furnaces of Bolckow & Vaughan, on 27 December 1897 – twin to her brother Edward and daughter of Mark and Margaret McKenna, formerly Quinn.

Above: Three young ladies take time to visit a studio in 1917. On the right is Katie Phillipson of Holden Street, who also worked on slag reduction at Bolckow & Vaughan's steel works, during the First World War. One of the girls on the left is Winnie Rushton of Pochin Road. She became the Matron at a Middlesbrough Hospital.

Above: Patrick O'Neill of Vaughan Street. Pictured far right with his comrades, Patrick O'Neill entered the war as a Bombardier in the Royal Engineers after an earlier three-year spell. He survived and spent some time after the war working as a labour recruit on the construction of the Middlesbrough to Redcar Trunk Road in the 1920s. He must have enjoyed the discipline of army life as he later joined the Territorial Army.

Right: The four generations in 1917. Four generations of one family were living in 98 Holden Street in 1917 when they decided to have their photograph taken 3 miles away in North Ormesby. Ellen Williams formerly White and née Ward (1836-1919) was born in Gateshead. Mary Jane Thomas, née White (1860-1937) was born in Whitwood and had thirteen children. Gwenllian McCarthy, née Thomas (1889-1950) was born in Grangetown and had five children. Johanna McCarthy (1915-1937) was born in Grangetown, married James O'Neill and died giving birth to her only child Patricia, who died two years later.

Upstairs and Downstairs. Following the long-established tradition of going into service or 'to place', many young ladies from Grangetown worked at the Adelphi Hotel in Harrogate during the Edwardian period. Pictured with hotel staff are Jane Anne Lively (front row, second left) and next to her Mary Burke (third from the left). Her sister Grace Burke is on the middle row fourth from the right. Anastasia Hanlon is on the same row fifth from the left. All came from Bessemer Street.

Mary Burke and Anastasia Hanlon. The young ladies of Bessemer Street are also pictured here seated together with a number of army personnel during the First World War period.

Above left: Mother and aunt in 1914. Seated in this poignant wartime studio portrait is Sarah Archbold née Simpson, mother of William H. Archbold on the left and Aunt to William Simpson of 96 Vickers Street, Grangetown, standing on the right. Her son William, 2nd-Lt of 228th field Coy, Royal Engineers, died on 21 October 1918, aged twenty-seven. He is buried at Lijsenthoek Military cemetery in Poperinge, Belgium. Her nephew William, a merchant seaman engineer survived to live a long life in Falmouth where he met his future wife.

Above right: The Murphy siblings in 1919. The Murphy family lived in Lackenby, South Bank and 95 Cheetham Street, Grangetown before they emigrated to Chicago in the 1920s. Pictured above are Joseph (who stayed in occupied Germany after the First World War, hence the uniform), his brother John who also served in the War, and their sister Catherine, who was a registered nurse.

Opposite above: The peace party in Stapylton Street in 1919. Originally assumed to be a coronation party in honour of King George V, we now believe this to be a party in honour of those who had close relatives who fought and died in the First World War. Doctor Steele's wife and her sister are cutting the cake. Sarah Wilkinson can be seen in the rear, to the right of the girl wearing a headband. She married William Herlingshaw of 102 Stapylton Street, pictured on the right in a light cap. He was a crane driver in the blast furnaces.

Opposite below: Grangetown Old Soldier Band in 1919. A battle-worn George Ayton of Grangetown stands behind the drum with fellow musicians after losing an eye during the First World War. They are pictured outside Marton Hall, once the home of the famous Henry Bolckow, just after the war had ended.

The Peace Festival Memorial in service 1919. Grangetown Peace Festival was held on Saturday 26 July 1919. A service was held in the Market Square at which the hymn 'All People That On Earth Do Dwell' was sung and a prayer by the Revd N.L. Fisher was said. Pte William Short's VC and memorial was referred to and was unveiled by Lt-Col B.M. Westerton, 8th Yorkshire Regiment. John Fox, Esq., J.P. County Councillor presided.

The Grangetown Silver Band. Always a regular source of entertainment for visitors, the Band was famous for its musical prowess and always let the town know how it had fared in any competition by playing 'Above the Waves of Earthly Strife' if it had won.

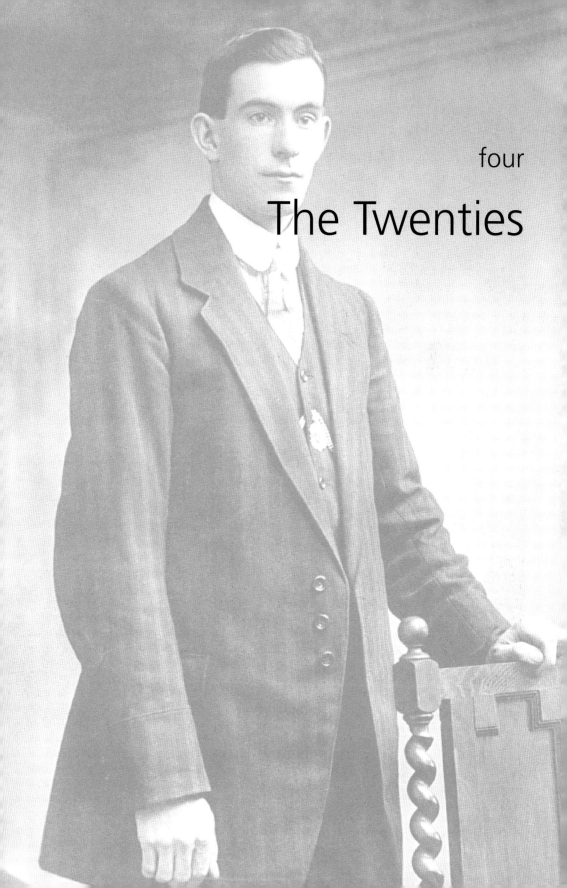

four

The Twenties

Above: St Mary's School Concert in 1920. From left to right, back row: -?-, Bridget Fox, Edna Devaney, Bridget McMahon, Madge Donnelly. Third row: Mary Barry, -?-, Mary Donaghy, Agnes Jarred, Mgt Conway, -?-, Mary McDonald. Second row: Timothy Twohig (the King), -?- (the Queen). Front row: Nancy/Lucy Fitzgibbon, Eileen Sullivan, Ellen McCarthy.

Left: Revd Fr Bernard Kelly in 1920. A popular parish priest of St Mary's in Grangetown from 1902 to 1928 and the founder and supervisor for the magnificent Church of Our Lady of Perpetual Help, built in 1905 for the families of the parish, Fr Kelly captured the heart of the children of the town with his generous nature, often handing out sweets and ice cream to little ones.

Grangetown Social Club Billiards Team and Committee in 1920. From left to right, back row: T. Barraclough, R. Allen, James Allen, John Allen, A. Bishop, J. Smith, D. Davies, W. Palmer, C. Wills, A. Lambton. Front row: W. Fisher, J. Russell, W. McLeod, J. Mardon, E. Lloyd, J.H. Burlison.

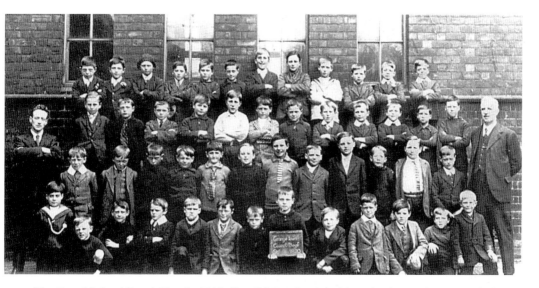

The Board School Boys' Class in 1920. 'Spoffy' Tombes is holding the slate and Ken Marshall is in the front row on the left wearing the sailor suit. Josiah Huss, the headmaster, is on the right. He was born in 1866, appointed in 1907 to supervise 443 students in six classrooms ranging from a minimum of fifty-four in Classroom One to a maximum of 115 in Classroom Six.

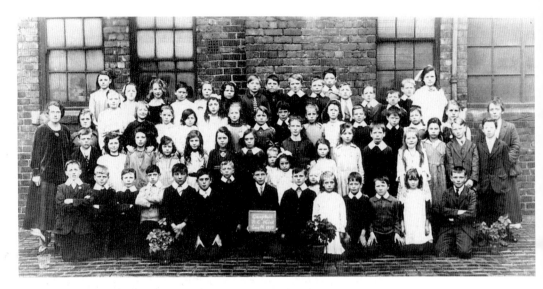

Grangetown St Mary's Mixed Group IV in 1920. From left to right, back row: Norah Shea, Lizzie Shea, C. Tierney, -?-, Cissie Doyle, Anna Murtha, ? Watson, R. Pearsall, ? Power, ? Burt, E. Healy, T. Redmond, J. Hayes, -?-, K. Jeffers. Third row: Mrs McNicholas, ? Devaney, ? Burt, ? O'Mara, ? Shea, ? Cronin, P. Lane, V. Jarred, T. McCarthy, ? Hayes, Lizzie Purcell, A. Shaughnessy, M.K. Bennett, J. Fleming, P. Devaney, Miss Brady. Second row: Celia O'Brien, May McMahon, ? O'Mara, ? McElvaney, B. Newton, D. Winn, Celia Rustin, A. Daly, -?-, W. Scott, F. Havelock, M. Donnelly, ? Fleming, G. Donnelly, -?-. Front row: John O'Neill, D. Duggan, Hughie McMahon, ? Meskill, M.K. McElvaney, M. Daley, P. O'Hagan,-?-, John Campbell, M. Walsh, L.A. Power, Tommy Havelock and -?-.

Grangetown St Mary's Mixed Group III in 1920. The back row includes M, Daly and J. Swan. In the third row are Timmy Linehan, John Traynor, Tommy Traynor, J. McNulty Joe Quinn, J. Fleming, ? Fleming and T. Devaney. In the second row are Kitty Redmond, ? Twohig, Margaret Twohig and ? Devaney. Alice Carr and Mary Carr are in the front row.

Grangetown St Mary's Mixed Group II in 1920. From left to right, back row: Jim McElvaney, Mary Barry, Mick Barry, Jim Cassidy, Sammy Smart, Jackie Walters, Gordie Hodgson, Jimmy Meskill, Jim McNulty, Nora McNulty, John Stuart, Harry Murtha, Stan Murtha. Third row: Pat McElvaney, Nellie Finn, Tom Cassidy, -?-, -?-, Barbie Hodgson, Tommy Scully, Peter Meskill, Mary McNulty, -?-, -?-, Mrs Caherty, ? Devaney. Second row: Katie Jeffers, Mattie Jeffers, Jimmy Finn, May Jeffers, Lizzie McGarrity, Sarah McGarrity, Delia Scully, Lizzie Freeman, Maggie Freeman, ? Doyle, -?-, and ? Devaney. Front row: the Watson sisters, Gerald Pyne, Mary Pyne, Katie Ryan, Winnie Ryan, Denis Couhig, John Couhig, ? Couhig, Eddie Gibbons?, Jimmy Foley, Francis Conway, Wilf Martin.

Grangetown RC Infants Group II in 1920. The teachers are Miss Kate Gribbin and Miss McNicholas. From left to right, back row: Mick Traynor, Eddie Doyle, Willie Hanlon, Willie Hanlon, Richard Foley, John Lagan, Frankie Morris, Jimmy Jones, Byrnes, Louie Ayres. Second row: Mary Fitzgibbon, Gertie Onion, Lizzie Lynd, Celia Ruddy, Johanna McCarthy, Sadie O'Brien, Doris Winn, Margaret Finn, Ellen Duggan, Barbara McNulty, Jimmy Murphy. Third row: Margaret Jones, Rachel Pedley, Cassie Conway, Winnie McCarthy, Bridget Ryan, Annie Kelly, Mary Farley, Winnie Traynor, Mary Garland, Mary Corcoran, Margaret Lawlor. Front row: Kittie Hanratty, Sarah McGarrity, Willie Meskill, Johanna McCarthy, Sarah Harrison, Mary Harrison, Ellen McNulty, Marie Carson, Hugh Carson, Gerard Pyne, Tommy McElhatton.

A 1920 wedding. Dai Thomas of 98 Holden Street returned from the First World War to marry Mary Ellen Welsh of 36 Bessemer Street in September 1920 in St Mary's church, Grangetown. His Best Man was his brother Dick Thomas and the Maid of Honour was Margaret Quinn. The bridesmaids were, from left to right: Winnie Traynor (standing) Maggie Lawlor, Cassie Bennett and Joanna McCarthy (standing). The couple, after losing their first child, emigrated to Chicago, USA, six years later with their two boys, to begin a new life. They had a daughter, Ellen, born in Chicago in 1930.

Sheaves and Corn Assembly at St Mary's School in 1921. From left to right, back row: Johanna McCarthy, Maggie Finn, Sarah McGarritty, Winnie Mohan, Mary Fitzgibbon, Doris Wynn, Margaret Jones, Jane O Sullivan. Middle row: Peggy Jones, Kitty Hanratty, Mabel Fitzgibbon, Joanne McCarthy, Winnie Traynor, Marie Carson, Philomena Jackson, Alice Carr, Mary Walsh, Renee Darragh, Cassie Bennett.Front row: Lil Murphy, ? McMahon, Biddy McMahon and Agnes Shipley.

St Matthew's football team in 1922. Pictured are players and trainers of the team, which included no less than four members of the Brooks family.

Grangetown Athletic Club in 1922. The young boy in front of Jim Thomas (fifth from the right on the back row) is the brother of Philomena Jackson, later Mrs Doran. He used to follow Jim everywhere. Standing second right (next to the tall chap in riding boots) wearing white shirt and dark tie is Walter Bird. The player, standing fourth left (first in the strip) is named Taylor.

St Mary's May procession, *c.* 1921. This was the first of many processions held by St Mary's parish after the First World War. It was held in honour of Our Lady, who, after appearing at Lourdes in 1858, also appeared to three children at Fátima in Portugal in 1917. This devotion to Mary continued until the 1970s and is still practised in a less spectacular form.

Above: St Matthew's Wolf Cubs in 1922. 'Chick' Maloney was the popular curate who guided the young boys of Grangetown in the ways of the Scout movement begun by Baden Powell in the Edwardian era. Grangetown's response to this remarkable new association was enthusiastic, as can be seen by the picture above.

Right: The Ward boys in 1922. Outside their family home, from left to right, are: William Ward (1917-1940) who was killed in action in France; George Herbert Ward (1911-2002), Evan Ward, Jack Ward and Robert Ward (1913-1995). Bob was a familiar figure employed as a manager in the Co-op Store in Whitworth Road.

Opposite below: Cleveland House and Fire Brigade, 1920s. A magnificent picture with a proud Fire Brigade attending the latest vehicles outside the recently acquired Council Offices.

Eston Sanatorium (The Fever Hospital), *c.* 1925. This primitive wooden building served the needs of the Grangetown and Eston communities from very early days. A local resident, Gwen Wadwell, formerly Watson, recalls how, as a child she used to scoot up the Eston Road from Bolckow Terrace every school lunch time in order to check on the progress of her sister Mary, convalescing there for six weeks with scarlet fever. A number on the board outside indicated how she and other patients were progressing with captions such as 'poorly', 'getting better' or 'needs visitors'. There were about fifty beds in total. Gofton Place now occupies the site.

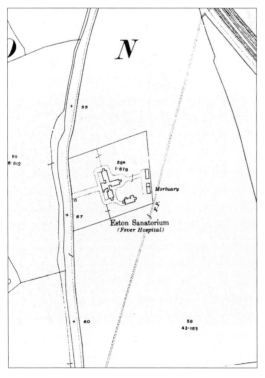

Left: A map of the hospital, *c.* 1900. *Right:* Gwen, aged nine years old.

An allotment garden in the early 1920s. This was probably opposite Vickers Street and features, from left to right: Margaret Annie Tonkin (1903-1984), Josiah Tonkin (1844-1927), young Eddie Tonkin and Elijah Tonkin, born in 1882.

The Duckering family allotment in Mushroom Grove was quite near their home in Bessemer Street. This photograph features, from left to right: an unnamed friend, Charles, Joan, Thelma and dad Charles. Allotments were a natural resource for families in this frugal time of high unemployment and low wages.

Above: St Mary's Parish Outing in 1924. A wonderful group photograph, possibly taken at York, of the ladies of the parish. Included are two nuns whom we suspect are Sisters Vincent and Mary who arrived 1920s to work in Grangetown. Faces recognized are Mrs Ryan, Mrs O'Sullivan, Mrs Gill, Mrs Rowden, Mrs Jane Burke, Mrs Mary Ellen O'Neill, Mrs Rooney and James Rooney, Mrs Margaret Conway, Mrs Bridget Fox, Mrs Margaret Dooley and Mrs Mary Traynor.

Above: A funeral cortège, 1920s. Seated in the first horse-drawn cab, William Turner of Victoria Road in Grangetown displays his tremendous collection of carriages and horses prior to the funeral.

Right: The British Legion Hut in Victoria Road, 1920s. Captured on camera are the steward and stewardess of Grangetown British Legion Club and members of the Committee.

Opposite below: Grangetown St Mary's Championship School Team of 1924. The adults on the left are J. Conway and the popular curate Revd Fr M. McEldowney. On the right are Jim Mannix and Pat Collins. Players in the back row, from left to right, are: Joe Quinn, Pat Daly and Jim Fitzgibbon. Middle row: Arthur Evans, Jim Dooley, Billy Murtha, Hughie McMahon and Mick Bennett. Front row: T. Devaney, J. McNulty, and Jack Fleming. Hugh McMahon turned professional in later years and played for Sheffield Wednesday and Sunderland FC.

~ GRANGETOWN SONGSTERS ~

Above: Salvation Army Singers in 1927. From left to right, back row: B. Jackson, R. Gibson, E. Dawkins, A. Becker, J. Bullock, J. Watson. Middle row: Mrs L. Hudson, Mrs McKie, Mrs Garbutt, Bandsman T. Tary, Mrs Kirk, Mrs Darbyson, Mrs Adams, Mr Coates. Front row: Mrs Thomas, ? Benton, ? Evans; Sqn Ldr Williams, Capt. Mussett, Dep Gen. Garbutt, Mrs Aungers, Mrs Tary, Mrs Richardson.

Left: Joseph Murphy of Cheetham Street. Like many others during these hard times, Joseph emigrated to Chicago in the 1920s with his parents, where he met and married his future wife. He regaled his son Kevin with tales of 'fires in the sky', having never forgotten his experiences here.

Left: Patrick Burke of Bessemer Street in 1928. Patrick emigrated to Canada in the late 1920s hoping to settle there and start a new life. He found things very hard in those early years and admitted in later life that he deeply regretted leaving Grangetown. His sister Mary, however, emigrated to Canada with her husband Tom to join Patrick with the intention of going over the border into America. This they did. They found work in the steelworks and that was the beginning of a dream come true for them. As Patrick established himself in the USA, his girlfriend Doris, also of Grangetown, emigrated to the USA, where they were married. The two couples worked together, became very prosperous and lived in Wyndotte, Michigan all their lives.

Right: Vaughan Street's cousins in 1925. John O'Neill and Thomas Doyle pose outside the back door of their home in Vaughan Street. Both left Grangetown during the Depression of the 1930s to seek employment in the London area. John worked for Fords Motor Works in Dagenham and married a childhood sweetheart Winnie Traynor in Barking, Essex. He returned with his young family at the outbreak of the Second World War.

Left: Gala Day in 1928. Children were not the only ones to dress up for this spectacular occasion. Here we have 'gypsy' mother Mrs Lambton and son Raymond 'Dick Turpin' in the yard of St Mary's School in Cheetham Street.

Below: Whitworth Road in 1928. A tram waits in the square for passengers to travel to North Ormesby via South Bank. The first tram was seen in the area in 1919. It remained a distinctive feature of the local landscape until the last trolley was discontinued in 1971.

Above: Market Square and Tram in 1928. Perhaps this is the same tram close up, where Patrick Golden (1865-1931) poses between driver and conductor.

Below: Roseberry Terrace, *c.* 1928. The Terrace was known to later residents as Bolckow Road. On the right is St Matthew's church, its spire behind.

The back of Bessemer Street, *c.* 1928. From left to right are Thelma, Charles, Joan Duckering and their neighbour Gavin Burke.

The Cyclops Locomotive. Dorman & Long & Co.'s Cleveland Steelworks Cyclops Loco had a reputation for being kept scrupulously clean by one-man, its driver George Prosser.

Above: Cleveland Works in 1929. Taken at about the same time that Bolckow & Vaughan relinquished the firm to Dorman & Long. Two workers, dwarfed by gigantic machinery, are engaged in punching fishplates.

Right: The Paragon Picture Theatre in 1929. Situated near the Mechanic's Institute, this corrugated structure was the regular choice of entertainment to which the people of Grangetown flocked. On certain occasions, children were admitted for free to read the subtitles to their older relatives. Wearing a bowler hat is the manager Mr Leo Vincent Martin, a renowned piano teacher. He is seen here with his helpers.

Jack and Ethel Dalton of Grangetown. Ethel married Mr John Dalton, an ex-chauffeur from Harrods of Manchester in 1915 after being widowed in 1912. Her surname was Ross when she was born in Eston Junction. She moved to Salford before eventually returning to Grangetown to open the confectionery shop (below), situated at 9 Whitworth Road. The shop opened in the late 1920s and served the people of Grangetown for over a decade. In the doorway are Jack Dalton, his daughter Kathleen and Miss Jo Fox, wearing the hat.

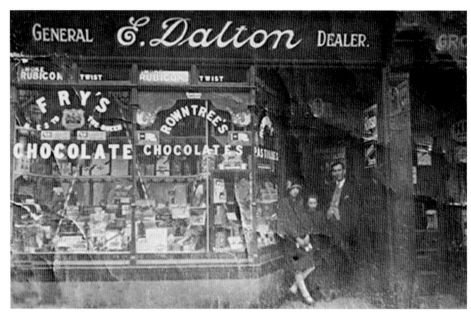

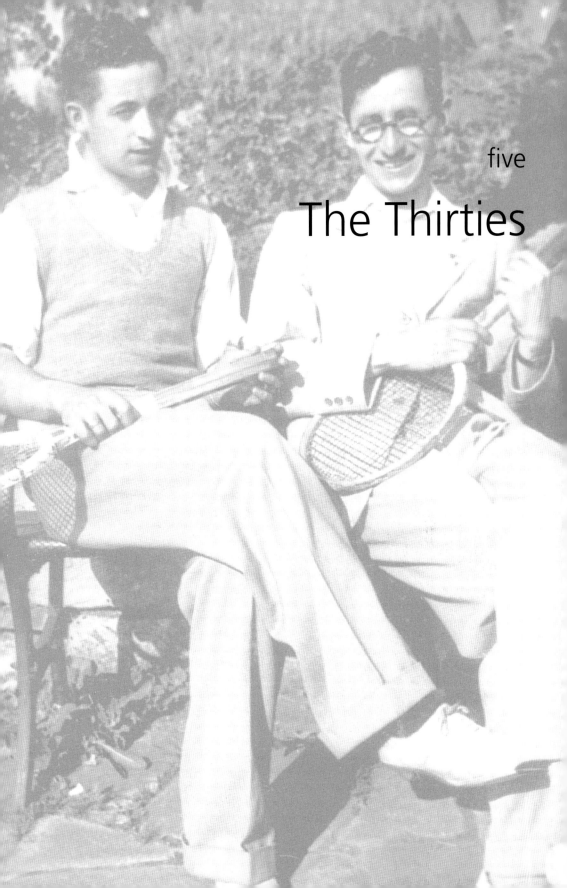

five

The Thirties

Above: Grangetown Mission Builders in 1930. From left to right, front row: Pastor Humphrey and Mr Sands, the secretary. Second row: Messrs Stubbs, Robinson, Sorrell, Pasby, Grievers, Richardson, ? Williams, J. Williams. Third row: Richardson, -? -, -?-, -?-, ? Beckett, ? Williams, L. Smith, ? Williams. Fourth row: -?-, Messrs Dawson, Dowing, Little, Davies, Prince, Suggett, Harrison. Fifth row: Messrs Morrison, Harrison, Vinter, Harrison, Ward, Green, Husband, Tonkin. Sixth row: Messrs Hall, Ward, Crosby, Longstaffe, Pattison, Taylor.

Left: Pastor Humphreys became one of the most respected men in Grangetown. He arrived as a young man in the early 1920s and from the 'Upper Room', above a stable in Whitworth Road, inspired people to build and develop a devout Christian community. Amidst a serious depression, with prayer and hard work, he led a zealous flock to build and maintain a church that still continues to spread its Christian message among the people of the area.

The Championship Team of 1931. St Mary's School team proudly display their 'Stormer' and 'Walsh' trophies. From left to right, back row: Mr 'Bruiser' Cleary, James 'Sonny' Donaghy, Pat Golden, Lol Sullivan, M. Cleary, Norman Cassidy, Victor or Leo McCreton, Canon English, Mr Daly. Middle row: Francis Daly, Billy Meskill, John Jones, Tony McElvaney, Gerry Nesbitt. Front row: Brian Cave and Gerard Fleming.

The Championship Team of 1933. St Mary's repeated the feat, wearing brand new strips in a brand new school building. Notice the backdrop of the 'farm school' wall. The recently appointed head teacher, Peter Mahon, on the right and the deputy head, Leo Wilkinson, on the left.

The Soup Kitchen, *c*. 1932. This gesture to the hungry children of Grangetown was made by volunteers who probably remembered the Durham strike of the 1890s where a similar kitchen was organized in the Board School playground.

Prince George's visit in 1933. Crowds gathered and old soldiers assembled to be inspected on the day that Prince George visited Grangetown's self-help programme of work.

The butcher's shop at 11 Whitworth Road, on the corner of Vickers Street, *c.* 1932. Proud owners Mr and Mrs Coates pose outside their establishment. In the 1950s it was more familiarly known as Roper's.

Bolckow Road and RC School, *c.* 1932. On the left are St Mary's School and church. There is no sign of the West Lane road although it ran parallel to Whitworth Road along the street gable ends to the works. Instead, we see a fence and notice board, which was probably used by the parish hall nearby.

Bolckow Road facing west, c. 1932. A strangely deserted thoroughfare on the outskirts of town, Lanny's Ice Cream Parlour, with its familiar canopy, was a meeting place for young people for many years. It once hosted the dance bands of the day above the Lido Café on Saturday nights.

War Memorial and Birchington Avenue, c. 1932. Almost empty, the Avenue stretches to the Trunk Road where a low-slung building occupies the centre of the recently built council housing development initiated by Eston Urban District Council. The cenotaph, erected soon after the First World War, is always kept in fine condition even to the present day.

SEAMAN & SON,

GRAMOPHONE DEALERS.

NEWSAGENTS   FREE DELIVERY
CONFECTIONERS & TOBACCONISTS.

Buy Your Records
from us
Quick Service,
Our Motto.

We hold the Largest
Stock of Radio,
Broadcast & Perfect
Records in the District

6, WHITWORTH ROAD,
& MARKET PLACE,
GRANGETOWN. YORKS.

Seaman's Gramophone Shop. Seaman's of 6 Whitworth Road advertises its prolific output of the latest 78 rpm record samples, hot from the press, to cater for the new dance crazes of the 1920s and '30s practised in the halls of Grangetown and South Bank. The Co-op Hall in Normanby Road was a favourite venue for the young, often staying open into the early hours.

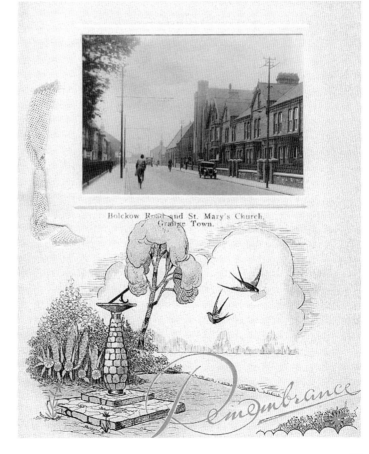

A Grangetown Christmas Card, 1930s.

Above: The Fox Family of Bolckow Road in 1936. Councillor Fox and his family pose outside their family home at No.36. From left to right, back row: James Fox (wearing a cap), Alice Fox, Jo Fox, Bill Fitzgibbon. Middle row: ? Fox, Bridget Fox *née* Quinn, Fr Michael Fox, Bridget 'Bee' Fox, John Fox. Front row: Patsy and Marie Fox.

Left: Anyone for tennis? Gavin Burke of Bessemer Street and Gerard Pyne of Cheetham Street pose for a snap as they wait for a game of tennis, possibly in the recently completed Eston recreation ground. This photograph was taken around 1935.

A Mission Trip to Saltburn, *c.* 1935. This is a fine picture of the Grangetown Mission members visiting Saltburn Social Centre. Mr Humphrey is in the centre of the front row, accompanied by a large and happy group. Others identified are Bob Green, Jim Humphreys and Mrs Farrer.

The Crusher Gang, *c.* 1935. Jim Keenan, pictured on the right of the front row, worked here as a teenager in the 1930s to ensure that the ore from Eston Hills was the right size to be used in the blast furnace process, further down the line.

Left: Coke Ovens, *c.* 1936. When Dorman, Long & Co. Ltd built and started to work these, many people nearby decided to leave for fresher pastures. The smell and pollution was intolerable.

Below: St Mary's Netball Team in 1935. This championship team includes Mary O'Neill, Mary Jones, Betty Rogers and Doris Onions. In the front row, from left to right, are: Annie McCarthy, Rita Conway and Winnie Shea.

St Mary's football team in 1935. From left to right, back row: Tom Hand, Billy Ferguson, J. Harrington, M. Cave, M. McNulty, D. McElvaney, -?-. Front row: J. Curtis, Albert Lanny, G. Power, A. McNicholas and P. Donaghy.

St Matthews Soccer Team, *c.* 1938. Churchwarden Bob Wanless of Eversham Road and Mr Brooks of Granville Road (tragically killed in the air raids of the Second World War) and Mr Smith are pictured here in a pre-war soccer team.

The Fox Children of Birchington Avenue in 1936. One of the first families to live in Birchington Avenue, Grangetown, the Fox family moved from South Bank in the early 1930s to occupy one of the newer houses built during this period of rapid housing development by the Eston Urban District Council. Standing from left to right are: James, Vincent, Michael and Imelda. Eugene is seated in the rocking chair. An enterprising travelling photographer, whose bicycle can be seen leaning on the fence behind, snapped a picture of them.

A coach trip from Market Square, *c.* 1935. Stylishly dressed ladies with large hand baggage pose before their journey. Fifth from left is Dickie 'Dye' Dawkins, before he became a famous businessman.

Sir William Worsley Council Senior School Staff, *c.* 1937. Opened in 1935, the staff included Head Teacher Mr E.S. Jackson and assistant teachers Messrs. R. Toomey, H. Stephens, R. Snow, J. Williamson, W. Jones, W. Palmer; Misses F. Jones, M. Baxter, M. Davies and M. Ferguson.

Left: The Lyric Cinema. Built in 1936 in the art décor style of the era, the Lyric cinema was the luxurious replacement for the tin-sheeted Paragon Cinema of the 1920s. It became a veritable haven for the local population who flocked to it in droves – especially when a Hollywood classic was promoted.

Below: Whitworth Road, *c.* 1935. Children spill out onto the main street outside the Board School oblivious to the possibility of a turning tram. On the left the new façade of Browns Furniture Shop can be seen. The shop replaced the Council Offices.

The Board School Staff. A happy group of females who presided over the education of children in the 1930s. The Headmistress was Connie Burns.

The boys and Sister Columba, 1939. From left to right, back row: Pat Cochrane, Kenny Davis, Sister Columba, Bill Terry, Jim Fox. Front pair: Bernard Mullen, John Grogan. Sister Columba appeared in a Movietone newsreel in Japan in the 1940s, after leaving Grangetown. The Lyric cinema, filled to capacity, heard her say, 'I am a nun and my name is Jean McBride.'

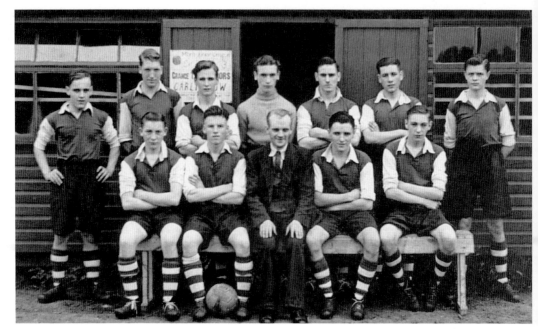

Grangetown Juniors Football Team in 1939. In a year or so, these young men would be engaged in military service with the town facing another war ending in a loss of more brave lives. Playing Carlin How on this day are, from left to right, standing on the back row: ? Watson, George King, Joe Scully, Jim Rooney, -?-, ? Marsh, Harry Tindall. Front row: ? Campion, ? Watson, Lenny Bugg (trainer), ? Jones, Jimmy Cave.

The Back Arch, 1930s. Here is a familiar scene from Grangetown's past, where a happy family enjoys the sun in the 'Back Arch' – the alley which runs between two streets.

six

The Second World War

Left: Land Girl finds love, 1943. One of the many Grangetown girls who did their bit for King and Country was Joan Dalton of Victoria Road, who, whilst working on a farm in the Guisborough area, lifting hay ready for baling with a pitchfork, accidentally flung a brick which hit a man on the head nearby. This man, obviously stunned in more ways than one, was to become her husband. His name was Joseph Tyerman and he left his farm in Hinderwell to marry Joan in 1946 and to work in Dorman and Long's steelworks at Grangetown.

Spitfire pilots training in Rhodesia. A Spitfire pilot in the Second World War, Jim Rooney of Cheetham Street crossed the Channel several times on special flying missions. Third from the left, Jim relaxes with other members of the squadron in Mount Hampden, Rhodesia, where he spent six months training. Others in the photograph include the pilots Bert Hinchcliffe of Dewsbury, George Sanderson of Ayr and far right, Frank Morgan of Wales.

Above left: The McElvaney Brothers. Henry and Isabella McElvaney of Birchington Avenue lost two sons in the Second World War. Dominic Anthony McElvaney (wearing a fez) of the Royal Horse Artillery Regiment was twenty-one years old when he was killed in action on Friday 21 November 1941 against Rommel's Afrika Corps in North Africa. He is buried in the Knightsbridge War Cemetery 25km west of Tobruk, Libya.

Above right: His brother Ronald, then only aged twenty-two, an Able Seaman in the Royal Navy was also killed in action when his ship the HMS *Capel* was torpedoed by a German U Boat on Boxing Day 1944 whilst escorting an American Convoy through the Scapa Flow bound for Russia. Ronald's body was never found. HMSs *Capel* and *Affleck* were actually chasing a U-boat (off Cherbourg, France) which, two days earlier, had sunk a troop ship, the SS *Leopoldville* with the loss of 763 Americans GIs. The u-boat U 486 captained by Oblt. Gerhard Meyer sank both British ships.

Right: Their brother James McElvaney of the Green Howard's regiment was also involved in those battles in North Africa. Fortunately, James, who was captured, managed to escape and survived the war. He went on to become the father of ten children.

Above: Ladies at War. For the second time in a century, war necessitated the introduction of women into the steel industry as men again left to join the forces after the declaration of war in 1939. Many were employed in the steel mills as they increased production to cater for the needs of war.

Left: Two ladies and their uniformed partners are snapped at Redcar in November 1942. On the left are Peggy Donnelly and Buddy O'Neill.

Army Group. This large group of soldiers pose in the Grangetown Board School.

Balloon Crew. Joan Duckering (left, back row) of Bessemer Street joined the WRAF and worked on balloons.

Above: Nurses at War, *c.* 1942. This St John's Ambulance Team of volunteer first aid nurses based in Eston during the war won a rose bowl for their efforts in a local competition. They include, from left to right, a retired nurse, Eliza Anne 'Lally' Williams, formerly Watson, her sister Elsie May English, Olive Hall and an unknown member.

Right: Thelma Duckering, *c.* 1943. Born at 77 Bessemer Street in Grangetown in 1918, Thelma left home at the age of fourteen to work as head housemaid at the home of a wealthy mill owner in Rochdale. In 1940, she joined the WRAF. After a couple of postings in the UK, Thelma was posted to Egypt. In Cairo she carried out an important role as a radio operator and also met and married her future airman husband, Ray. They returned to Rochdale after the war and have always paid frequent visits to Grangetown throughout their lives.

Left: The Ayton Brothers. This photograph, taken on 30 July 1940, is of the Ayton brothers who all lived at 112 Vickers Street before the war and later in Shakespeare Avenue. Standing at the back is Edward James Ayton (Jim) who was born in Eston in 1907. He served in the Norfolk Regiment and was eventually taken as a prisoner-of-war by the Japanese. Jim did not have the best of wars, having also suffered the evacuation from Dunkirk. After his capture by the Japanese, Jim spent time in Changi and worked on the Burma Railway; conditions on that project are well publicised. It is said that because he played the bugle, it saved his life; the bugle was the means of communication between the Japanese and prisoners and because of this he was considered less disposable. He was nevertheless left with splinters in his spine, a hernia and malaria. Jim married Emily Ankers and worked as a bread deliveryman with Welford's Bakery in Redcar.

Seated on the left is Robert William Ayton (Rob) who was born in Vickers Street in 1918. He served with the Royal Engineers. Rob spent part of the war in the desert of Basra. He was in Europe after D Day and saved the lives of a mother and daughter in Germany. After the war, he married Alma Ash. He worked as a crane driver at the works.

Front right is George Albert Ayton who was born at 112 Vickers Street on Boxing Day in 1919. He served in the Royal Scots and was billeted in South Shields where he met his future wife. He was involved in the D Day Landings and was in an explosion in which thirty-nine of his comrades died. He left the army in 1946 and worked for a time as a caretaker in one of the schools in Grangetown before moving to South Shields where he settled.

Right: The Herlingshaw Brothers in 1943. A rather strange coincidence during the war led to Bill Herlingshaw of Stapylton Street and his brother Raymond accidentally meeting in Durban South Africa whilst on active service. This photograph is the result.

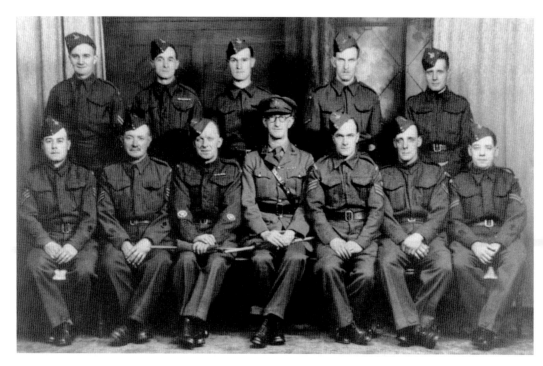

A wartime scene in Belgium in 1944. George Ayton and his comrades survey the dereliction and destruction of a town in Belgium during the Second World War. None of his comrades survived.

Bill Burke, c. 1943. Bill Burke of Bessemer Street enjoys a wartime excursion in a motorcycle and sidecar.

Above: Thomas Cave of Laing Street. Ordinary Seaman Thomas Cave P/JX380705 who served on the HMS *Collingwood* died of wounds received on the ship on Wednesday 8 March 1944 whilst on a training exercise.

Right: Jack Doyle of Vaughan Street. Able Seaman Jack Doyle served on the HMS *Chamois* as a stoker for three years in Icelandic waters and later on the HMS *Fairy*. He was blown off his bunk once when a mine struck the ship and suffered minor injuries. Other ships in the flotilla suffered more serious losses near Blyth. He participated in the D-Day landings and when asked what his favourite food was, replied, 'Rum!' A portion of this was enjoyed daily by all.

Above: A Crew in Gibraltar, *c.* 1945. Ken Lightfoot, proprietor of the Lightfoot newsagency of Whitworth Road is seen with his comrades-in-arms enjoying a spell of Mediterranean sunshine. He is third from the right in the middle row. He inherited the ever-familiar shop, along with his brother Bill, from his father 'Geordie', who, in turn, inherited it from his mother. She established the business in Bessemer Street in the early 1900s. Ken and his brother Bill expanded the business by operating other premises in Whitworth Road and Bolckow Road.

Left: Boiler yard Workers, *c.* 1944. Taken in about 1944, this photograph shows a group of men from the Boiler yard fabrication shop of Dorman, Long & Co. Cleveland relaxing in their lunch break. Included in the picture are: John O'Neill (in the beret) and John Jones (front right) with their fellow workers.

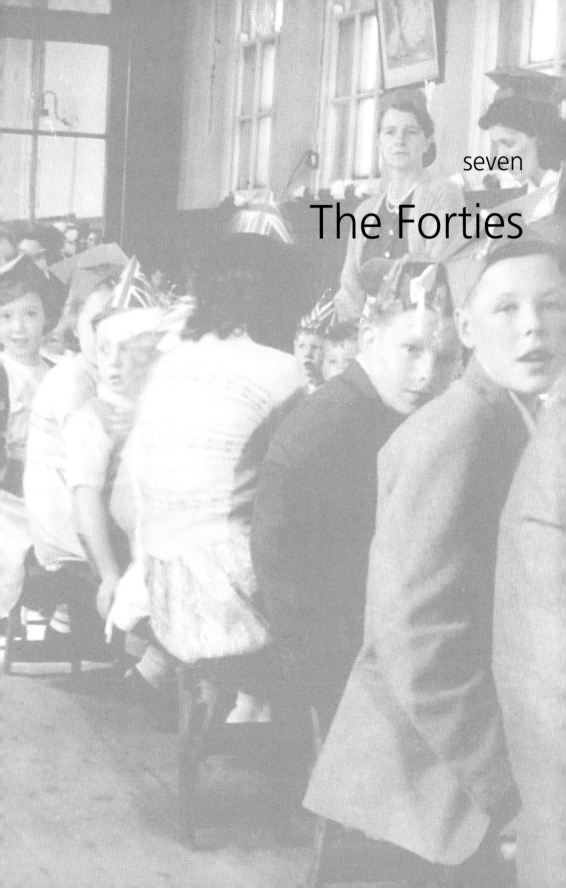

seven

The Forties

Board School Shield Winners in 1940. Set against the familiar background of the Eston Hills, Hilda Best (an apt name!), on the left, enjoys the moment of knowing that their team is the best in the area.

St Peter's School prefects in 1942. These were the first ever prefects of St Peter's Senior School which had only just opened when this photograph was taken in January 1942. On the back row, far right is Michael Fox, who was a fitter at Dorman & Long's steelworks.

Above: A peace party in 1945. School children are seated in St Mary's Infant School hall for the peace party to celebrate the ending of the Second World War. Harry Fennon is seated second from the right.

Right: Evans Street in 1948. A baby is held by a family friend against the familiar backdrop of a distant Grangetown steelworks, the Lyric Cinema and Brown's cycle shop. The baby is Elaine Tyerman of Victoria Road and the lady is Madge Taylor of Lazenby.

Above: Silver Jubilee Celebration, *c.* 1945. Fr McEldowney, the parish priest of St Mary's for fifteen years celebrates his Silver Jubilee with the ladies of the parish. Behind him is Revd Fr Francis O'Hara and alongside him, Mrs Rynn.

Opposite above: An aerial view of the River Tees and town in 1946. An impressive panoramic view captures the relationship of a town, river and hills surrounded by fumes filling the sky before the imposition of smoke control emissions in the 1960s.

Opposite below: The Ayton's of Shakespeare Avenue, *c.* 1948. George is seated here with his wife and daughters outside their home in Shakespeare Avenue.

St Peter's Senior School girls enjoy a trip to Bowes Museum, *c.* 1947. Among those recognised are Joan Whiles, Mary Mannix, Katherine Livingstone, June Havelock, Pat Harrison, Betty Igo, Connie Harrison, Pat Healy and Sheila Larkin.

Pochin Road Group in 1947. Brian Buggey and John Short are holding a tray, and Jeanette Child has a basket. Beryl and Ann Baxter are both kneeling, Barbara Hannah is holding a clock, Jimmy Haggarth has a chef's hat; Jean Turner holds a rolling pin, and Ann Waugh has a mixing bowl.

Board School boys in 1947. A tremendous post-war school photograph with many familiar names. From left to right, back row: G. Cranwell, K. Milsom, R. Heath, J. Collins, G. Duffield, Duncan McKenzie. Middle row: G. Hunt, Jim Keenan, R. Hewling, J. Prout, R. Jefferson, Dave O Connell, -? -, G. Cooper, R. Spavin. Front row: K. Wright, R. Irons, -?-, K. Boggett, -?-, -?-, J. Leach, G. Collins, F. Cowell, and the teacher, Mr Dunn.

St Mary's Fourth Year Junior class in 1949. From left to right, back row: Mr Mahon, the head master, Arthur Evans, Tony Long, ? Bartley, Jimmy Power, Ronnie Wild, Ronnie Harrison, Charlie Littlewood, Tommy Quinn, Jimmy Turner, Clem Pattison. Third row: Mary Havelock, Maureen Thickett, Noreen Snowball, Theresa Craddy, Joyce Danby, Kathleen Kirkbright, Maureen Couhig, Gerard Hooper, Maureen Carr, Michel Wilkinson. Second row: Brian McMullen, Sheila McPhillips, Brian O'Neill, Olwynn French, Irene Hetherington, Maureen Martin, Rose Murphy, Sheila Wilkinson, Pat Chedzey. Front row: Bernard Igo, Peter Wrigglesworth, Brian Gallagher, Tony Collins and Tommy Summerhill.

Above: Forties fashion, *c.* 1949. After the privations of the war, Enid Nelson, her friend Alice, and Victoria and Betty Ayton of Vickers Street pose in typical forties attire before enjoying an evening's entertainment. Betty and her friends worked at the munitions factory in Newton Aycliffe during the war, travelling by the early morning train.

Right: Jim Keenan and his uncle, *c.* 1948. Nephew and uncle demonstrate the latest fashion in trench coats.

A mission trip to Stokesley in 1949. The ladies of Grangetown Baptist church pose outside one of Turner's coaches in 1949. In the forefront, Pastor Humphreys and driver Bill, playfully wear headgear in keeping with the present company.

Ayton family group on the doorstep of their Shakespeare Avenue house, c. 1947. From left to right: Alice Bates (née Ayton), Maggie Ayton (née Buxton), Paul Bates and Betty Ayton. Behind is Emily Ayton (née Ankers).

Grangetown Boys' Club London visit, *c*. 1948. From left to right, back row: Harry Anderson, Dick Thomas, Les 'Pop' Roberts, Ian Lanchester, ? Richardson, -?-, John Downes, Alf Bowker. Middle row: Colin Hutchinson, Alan Thompson, Charlie Smales (Club Leader), George Himsworth, Tommy Byrne, George Jackson, Frank Hardisty. Front row: Mick Kidger, -?-, Frank Waller, Gerard Bruen and ? Appleyard.

Grangetown Boys' Club Camp in 1949. Situated in Scalby, the now-famous Boys' Club Camp, under the respected and popular Charles Smales, introduced hundreds of youngsters to camp craft skills over many years. The 'Boss', as he was affectionately known, is fourth left on the back row. From left to right, back row: Sam Pearsall, Alan Baxtram, Alf Bowker, Charlie Smales, Ian Lancaster, Vin Noteyoung, -?-, Richard Thomas. Middle row: Jim Fox and Walter Patchett. Front row: George Lupton, Jackie Mannix, Gully Binns, R. Gibson, Bernard Mullen, Billy Hardisty, Johnny Stubbs and Dave Smales.

eight

The Fifties

Above: Trolley bus in Market Square, *c.* 1950. The original route from North Ormesby to Grangetown had a spur from Bennett's corner in South Bank. The wires were extended from Grangetown to Kingsley Road in 1950 and again with the increased housing development in 1964.

Left: St Mary's church, *c.* 1950s. Built in 1905, the name of the church was Our Lady of Perpetual Succour – the letters engraved in stone around the entrance archway.

Left: Lanny's Corner, *c.* 1952. A trio of girls pause before Lanny's Lido Café and an impressive low slung car parked outside.

Below: The Blacksmith's shop, *c.* 1954. The foreman, Mr Binks, seen wearing his cap, enjoys a joke whilst posing with workmates in Cleveland's Works. Third from the right is Bob Duckering, and Dick Coleman is also present.

Board School Girls 1A in 1951. From left to right, back row: Lillian Green, -?-, Elaine Jones, -?-, Scott ?, Caroline Hare, Gillian Dennis, Wendy Best, Maureen Cooper, Dorothy Crisp and ? Thomas. Middle row: -?-, Ann Carman, Sylvia ?, -?-, Iris Frost, Carol Buxton, -?-, Marian ?, -?-, Margery ?. Front row: Yvonne Everson, -?-, Gloria Robinson, -?-, -?-, teacher Miss Johnson, Sandra ?, Pauline Burke, -?-, Rita Cliffe, Mary Ward.

St Peter's School Choir in 1951. The music teacher, Joe Mullen, is seated with a large group of pupils. He was the inspiration behind all the choirs of this period.

Sir William Worsley class in 1955. From left to right, back row: Norman Crowther, Kenneth Patterson, Malcolm Bareham, Kenneth Bourne, Peter Orton, Alan Nixon, Barry Milsom. Middle row: Maurice Newton, Clive Cable, Brian Foreman, Doreen Cotty, Sheila Craven, Margaret Lewis, Lilian Hardy, Barbara Hannah, Jean Turner, Beryl Cook, Bernard Reeve, Barry Large, Ivan Huddlestone, Harold Hobson. Front row: Carol Woolstone, Janet Speakman, Margaret Pickthall, Dorothy Willett, Maureen Errington, Ann Cook, Mr Wyndham Jones, Ann Herlingshaw, Mary Patchett, Valerie Smith, Ivy Bassett, Valerie Johnstone and Ann Short.

St Peter's Class of 1956. From left to right, back row: Terry 'Dicky' Bird, Tony Hetherington, Brian Smurthwaite and Stanley Robson. Middle row: Walter Daley, Pat Havelock, Joan Sullivan, Kathleen Wagner, Pat Oxbury, Barbara Livingstone, Margaret McNicholas, Linda Reed, Anne Clark, Isolde O'Neill, Pauline Henzel, Margaret Cholmondely, Tony O'Hagen. Front row: Anne Hudson, Albert Humphreys, Bernadette Pickering, Tommy Duggan, Doreen Watts, Anne Donnelly, the teacher Miss Mossey, John Quinn, Kathleen Ginty, Patrick Harford, Mary Russell, John Williamson, Cynthia Cunningham.

Adult residents of Lee Road pose in party hats to celebrate the Coronation of Queen Elizabeth II in 1953.

Children of the above pose in St Matthew's garden. Recognised are Paul Fox, Vincent O'Neill, and brothers Michael and Hugh Wilkinson.

Teddy Boys, *c.* 1958. This photograph appears to be of a rock group from the era. They look suitably 'cool' with Billy Fury/Elvis lip curls in evidence and Tony Martin dressed in a white sports coat (full drape) with a pink carnation! From left to right, back row: Derek Cassidy, Freddy Hughes, Bud Ditchburn, Ginger Iseton, Hugh Bartley, Albert Humphries, Tony Martin, Jacky Towell. Front row: -?-, Albert Watson, Malcolm Roberts.

Sharman and Elaine in 1955. In the distance we can see Davison's Corner Shop and Argyle Road houses facing Victoria Road and in the foreground a bemused boy, hands in pockets, watching the photographic action perhaps after staring at the bicycles in Brown's shop window opposite. Elaine Tyerman of Victoria Road is just seven years old.

A day at the races in the 1950s. Members of St Mary's Social Club pose happily in front of their coach before a trip to the Ebor at York. From left to right: Tommy Traynor, Brian Cave, Johnny Traynor, Joe O'Neill, Johnna McAuliffe, -?-, Mick Traynor. Eddie Hoggett is at the coach window.

Blackpool in 1956. Blackpool was a favourite holiday venue for many at this time, especially for the young people of Grangetown. Pictured outside their regular Guest House are, from left to right, back row: Alan Lincoln, Jim Fox, Robbie Speakman, Eugene Fox, Bill Evans. Front row: Jeff Johns, Colin Joy.

Grangetown Boy's Club's annual Christmas party, 1955. Dignitaries include Councillors Hodgson, Herlingshaw, Dr Mackay, Leader Charles Smales, pictured with their wives and helpers and members at their yearly get-together.

St Mary's first-year class, 1956: a smiling class of thirty-nine pupils with their teacher, Mrs Mannix.

St Mary's School, c. 1956. A happy bunch of children are pictured inside the classroom with their teacher Mr Graham.

Grangetown Boys' Club Championship Soccer Team, *c.* 1950. From left to right, back row: E. Duckett, H. Anderson, L. Willis, L. Haverson, R. Nelson, N. Clark, K. Hindmarsh, M. Ewbank, Doug Cooper. Front row: J. McPhillips, V. Noteyoung, S. McPhillips, J. Noteyoung, N. Coyle Leader Charles Smales, and his unknown assistants.

Alderman William Jones' Soccer Team in 1957. Built in 1953, the school became a popular, thriving educational establishment. From left to right, the photographed people are: Stephen Skelton, Brian Parsons, Neil Robinson, George Agar, Bill Herlingshaw, Stewart Pearson, Peter Colony and headmaster Horace Duck.

The King's Head Hotel, *c*. 1960s. On the corner of Victoria Road and Evans Street, the Kings Head, sometimes know as the 'Top' House, stands strangely alone as if remembering its glory days, when it satisfied the needs of thirsty steelworkers of the past. It sadly had to be demolished after a fire in the latter part of the twentieth century.

Birchington Avenue. In the distance beyond the famous Bull Ring lies the Eston Hills, the reason for Grangetown's industrialisation and eventual wealth; John Vaughan discovered the seam of ironstone which led to the development of the steel industry in such magnitude.

An aerial view of Grangetown in the 1960s. A view of the extent of Grangetown's development since Victorian times. From the iron and steel works of the north alongside the River Tees, the new housing of the 1960s stretches southwards to be absorbed by the nearby Eston Hills.

Other local titles published by Tempus

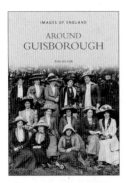

Around Guisborough
PAM WILSON

This collection of over 200 archive photographs portrays life in and around the town of Guisborough during the last 150 years. The images reveal the gradual physical change in the buildings and streets, from the opening of garages and petrol stations to children playing in fields which now house new generations of Guisborians. Horse-drawn vehicles, charabancs, annual carnivals as well as the people themselves are also remembered.
0 7524 3075 0

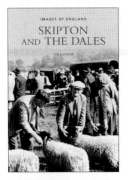

Skipton and the Dales
KEN ELLWOOD

Compiled by local historian Ken Ellwood, each of the 200 images included in this book offer a lasting pictorial record of this area over the last 150 years. Many details are examined, including schools, buildings, businesses and local characters. Also included are aerial photographs of this part of the Dales, and special attention is paid to the airmen from the villages around Skipton who lost their lives in the Second World War.
0 7524 3058 0

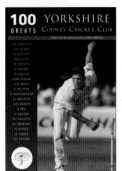

Yorkshire County Cricket Club 100 Greats
MICK POPE AND PAUL DYSON

The County Championship is the greatest cricket competition in the world. The fact that Yorkshire, with 29 titles, is pre-eminent in its history suggests that its Broad Acres have produced many great players. From George Anderson, who first played for Yorkshire in 1850, through to Matthew Hoggard, who received the coveted county cap in 2000, this book features 100 of the cricketers who have shaped Yorkshire CCC.
0 7524 2179 4

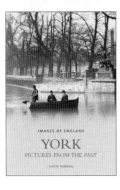

York: Pictures from the Past
YVETTE TURNBULL

Drawn from the archive held at York Central Library, these 200 photographs are accompanied by information and local stories which illuminate the city of York over the past 150 years. Through this book the reader will walk forgotten streets and meet people who lived in the city's historic heart or the less well known back streets. Other images include pleasure boating on the River Ouse and devastation caused by river floods that have plagued the city for years.
0 7524 3247 8

If you are interested in purchasing other books published by Tempus, or in case you have difficulty finding any Tempus books in your local bookshop, you can also place orders directly through our website
www.tempus-publishing.com